FRANKLIN ROOSEVELT

A Life From Beginning to End

Copyright © 2017 by Hourly History.

All rights reserved.

Table of Contents

Introduction
Sara Delano's Golden Boy
The Roosevelt Household: Son, Mother, Wife
Politics and Infidelity
Roosevelt, the Paraplegic
FDR Offers Americans a New Deal
Eleanor, the First Lady
The Arsenal of Democracy
The United States Enters War
The Death of the Longest Serving President
Conclusion

Introduction

America was still in its infancy when a political dynasty appeared. The Adams presidents, father and son, were followed by the Harrisons, William Henry and his grandson Benjamin, and the George Bushes are the most recent additions to the family combos. But these presidents are not among the top-tier occupants of the executive branch. Their names do not resound with the accolades of historians for their achievements as leaders. There was a family, however, whose representatives consistently rank among the best of American presidents. They came from two different branches of the family, and they represented different political parties, but both were imbued with an irrepressible sense of purpose and optimism that redefined their eras. The America that they led is still imprinted with the legacy of the Roosevelts.

The two Roosevelts, Oyster Bay branch's Theodore and Hyde Park's Franklin, were fifth cousins, and the families were split on their political affiliations. When it came to politics, family took a back seat, and throughout campaigns, the Roosevelts did not hesitate to back their party rather than their bloodlines. When it came time to marry, however, Franklin married his fifth cousin Eleanor, who was Theodore Roosevelt's niece. Theodore Roosevelt continued to be a role model for the younger Franklin, but for the man who would break traditions left and right, serving four terms when the tradition was half that, a different set of tools was needed for the task of repairing the United States.

Franklin Roosevelt came to power at a time when the United States was in the throes of the Great Depression. Franklin could not travel the nation to inspire Americans due to his disability, but no one was better at communicating his will, thanks to the use of his radio "fireside chats" and the mobility of his First Lady. Eleanor Roosevelt fought for union workers, African-Americans, women, and the poor as a tireless advocate of the downtrodden.

Members of Roosevelt's class despised him for what they regarded as his betrayal of the principles of the elite. Political enemies attacked him for the manner in which he expanded the powers of the presidency. But FDR was a fighter, and he took on all his naysayers with the same zeal that, after December 7, 1941, he would take on the Axis Powers in World War II. Americans voted him into office for four consecutive terms, knowing that, when FDR fought, America won.

Chapter One

Sara Delano's Golden Boy

"The highest ideal I could hold up before our boy (was for him) to grow up to be like his father, straight and honorable, just and kind, an upstanding American."

—Sara Delano Roosevelt

By the time James Roosevelt of the Hyde Park Roosevelts met Sara Delano, he was a widower with a secure position in New York society. From his first marriage to his second cousin had come a son, James Roosevelt, born in 1854. Four years after his wife's death, James attended the graduation party of his distant cousin Theodore Roosevelt, Jr. There he met Sara Delano, who was 26 years younger than he was, the same age as his son. But Sara, one of five sisters, was a strong woman whose devotion to husband James and son Franklin would be a crucial characteristic in the development of a future president.

The Roosevelt family's origins in New York began in the seventeenth century, when Claes Maartenszen van Rosenvelt, sometime between 1638 and 1649, arrived from the Netherlands. He purchased land a short time later in Manhattan, an area that today is the location of the Empire State Building. Son Nicholas changed the spelling of the surname to Roosevelt and began the family involvement in politics, serving as an alderman. It was from his sons that the two branches of the Roosevelt family emerged: Johannes began the Oyster Bay clan, which would eventually include Theodore Roosevelt, and Jacobus the Hyde Park branch, from which Franklin Roosevelt would spring. It would not be until the late nineteenth century that the families would be identified by their political ideology, as the Oyster Bay Roosevelts favored the Republican Party while the Hyde Park Roosevelts were Democrats.

That interest in politics characterized Franklin's great-grandfather, Isaac Daniel Roosevelt, who was a politician and a businessman. His son James Roosevelt, known as Squire James, born in 1828, pursued the family's business interests in coal and transportation and served as vice president of the Delaware and Hudson Railway and president of the Southern Railway Security Company. He also bred horses.

The Delano family was oriented toward business as well; Franklin's grandfather, Warren Delano, made a fortune in China's tea and opium trades, only to lose his fortune and make a second one. Sara had spent several years of her childhood in Hong Kong before returning to the family's estate on the Hudson River near Newburgh, New York. Most of her education came at home except for a brief period attending a girls' school in Germany.

Sara was tall, confident, and beautiful, and had her pick of suitors, but in 1880 she chose James Roosevelt to be her husband. The couple, who against the expectations of their families and their social circle were happily married, became parents when Franklin Delano Roosevelt, named for Sara's uncle Franklin Hughes Delano, was born on January 30, 1882. But the joyous occasion had a somber side when the doctors counseled Sara against bearing any more children. Had other children been born, Sara might not have been so absorbed in her only son's life, but instead, she took it upon herself to perform the duties of a mother which, in other affluent households, were left to a servant. Sara was fiercely proud of her son and said that "My son, Franklin, is a Delano and not a Roosevelt at all."

Summers and major holidays were spent in Massachusetts, where the Delano family had a home. During the rest of the year, Franklin grew up in a happy, privileged household on a large estate near Hyde Park, located fifty miles north of New York City. Both parents were greatly involved in their son's childhood, much more than was typical of parents in their social strata. In other ways, however, Franklin's life was much like that of scions of affluence in New York. From the age of two through fifteen, he traveled to Europe with his parents, becoming conversant in French and German. He learned to ride, row, play polo, golf and tennis, and shoot. His fondness for sailing was rewarded by a sailboat from his father when Franklin was 16 years old.

At the age of 14, Franklin was enrolled in Groton School, a private Episcopalian school attended by the sons of America's elite families. Headmaster Endicott Peabody believed that Christians had the responsibility to come to the assistance of others in need, a philosophy that he instilled in Groton students. The school, which was dedicated to training students to serve the public, was a challenging alternative to the nurturing home environment in which Franklin had received his early education. Franklin was not a standout athlete, a trait which the school revered, and so he did not become one of the most popular students. Nonetheless, Roosevelt was strongly influenced by Peabody, who would continue to be involved his life, officiating at his marriage and visiting him at the White House during his years as president.

In 1900, Franklin enrolled at Harvard College, but a few weeks into the school year, James Roosevelt, who had been weakening for the past decade, died from his heart problems. Sara moved to Boston while Franklin was at Harvard rather than be separated from her son.

Franklin became determined to be more successful at Harvard than he had been at Groton, although grades were not his primary emphasis. He graduated in 1903 but remained at Harvard as a graduate student. His extracurricular activities continued when he became the editor of the *Harvard Crimson*, the student newspaper. It was during his Harvard years that Franklin discovered his political identity as a Democrat, an interesting decision, considering that Theodore Roosevelt was the Republican president of the country at that time. Although Franklin admired his Oyster Bay kinsman's dynamic leadership, party trumped family, and Franklin campaigned for Roosevelt's opponent, William Jennings Bryant, during the presidential election.

In 1905, Franklin enrolled in law school at Columbia University although the law did not command his interest. He remained there for two years but dropped out before graduating. At this time, he was still searching for his direction in life. Neither he nor his mother would fully understand how much his future would depend upon Theodore Roosevelt's shy, unassuming niece, Eleanor.

Chapter Two

The Roosevelt Household: Son, Mother, Wife

"It is a good thing to keep the name in the family."

—Theodore Roosevelt

So far in his life, Franklin had failed to stand out in any endeavors or excel in any field which indicated a promising career. It could not be said that this lackluster profile came about because he was distracted by women. He was somewhat of a failure in terms of attracting the opposite sex. While he was at Harvard, he had proposed marriage to a 17-year-old Boston girl who refused him; at the time, Roosevelt was awkward around women, and the rebuff may have wounded his self-esteem.

But in 1902, while on a train, Franklin was reintroduced to his distant cousin Anna Eleanor Roosevelt, who was as serious as he was high-spirited. Franklin was not at ease around other women, but Eleanor was different. She was intelligent, shy and retiring, and charmed by her suitor. Eleanor had not grown up in the happy, supportive home that Franklin had enjoyed. Born in 1884, Eleanor had lost her mother and brother to diphtheria by 1892. In 1894, her father, who had been admitted to a sanitarium for his alcoholism, suffered a seizure when he jumped from a window during an attack of delirium tremens and died, leaving Eleanor an orphan.

Eleanor's early years did not benefit from the powerful, nurturing love that Franklin had known. Her mother, a society beauty, had called her daughter "Granny" because of her plainness. Her father had an illegitimate son from an affair with a servant in the household. She had gone to school in England, where she blossomed, learning French, becoming a popular member of the student body, and thriving under the tutelage of her headmistress. But in 1902, she was called back home so that she could make her debut, an experience that was excruciating for the 17-year-old Eleanor, who had lived abroad for so long that the other girls at the debutante balls were strangers to her.

But if she was socially maladroit, she already had a social conscience. As a member of New York's Junior League, she taught dancing and calisthenics in the slums of the East Side. Not everyone approved of the manner in which upper-class young women were adopting new roles in the new century; one of her male relatives decried the Junior League because it was encouraging women to engage in public activity. The life that Eleanor would lead in the years to come was very different from what was permissible for young ladies of good breeding, but the awkward debutante would become a trailblazer for her gender in the future.

Franklin's mother, who had hopes of having her son to herself for a few years before he left to become a husband, had not encouraged any of her son's romances. For a while, the romancing Roosevelts kept up a covert correspondence, revealing to no one that they were falling in love. They became engaged on November 22, 1903, but Franklin's relationship with Eleanor remained stealthy, even to the extent of using a private code in his diary when writing about Eleanor.

In 1904, Franklin finally disclosed to Sara that he and Eleanor were in love and planned to get married. Franklin's mother had no objection to Eleanor except her youth; Eleanor was only 19, Franklin 21, and she told the couple that they needed to postpone their plans to marry for a year. Franklin understood the depth of his mother's reaction and admitted in a letter that he knew he had caused her pain. But he stuck by his decision, saying that he knew his mind and it wasn't going to change. Sara was determined to try. With the idea of parting the two young lovers, Sara took Franklin on a Caribbean cruise. Distance and delay, despite Sara's hopes, failed to change her son's intentions.

The wedding was set for March 17, 1905, because it was convenient for the man who was going to give the bride away. Already scheduled to attend New York's St. Patrick's Day Parade, President Theodore Roosevelt would then fill the role of father for his favorite niece at the wedding, giving the bride away in marriage and signing the marriage certificate. Because of the presence of the president, the union made the front page of *The New York Times*.

Soon, Sara found a solution to the problem of acclimating to a daughter-in-law. She built a double townhouse in Manhattan: one side was for the newlyweds, the other side for herself, and there was a sliding door in between the two residences. The house was decorated and furnished by Sara with input from Franklin. Eleanor's preferences were not sought. For a shy young woman, the presence of a confident, dominating mother-in-law who was so plainly focused on her son did nothing to strengthen Eleanor's frail self-esteem.

The first baby, daughter Anna Eleanor, was born the year after they were married, and the son James arrived the following year. Sara was as engrossed in her grandchildren as she was in her son, and she had no qualms about imposing her views on child-rearing upon husband and wife. Emotionally distraught after giving birth to two children in two years and dealing with a domineering mother-in-law, Eleanor had an emotional breakdown. Even a strong woman who was secure in her identity would have struggled with a mother-in-law like Sara, who undermined Eleanor's role as a parent, at one point telling the Roosevelt children, "Your mother only bore you; I am more your mother than your mother is."

Eleanor told her husband that she didn't like living in a house that represented someone else's taste and preferences and was not hers in any way. Nor did she particularly enjoy the sexual intimacy of marriage, regarding it with the Victorian attitude that intercourse was something that women had to endure. Quite the opposite of her mother-in-law, who had relished caring for her son, bathing him and reading to him when he was an infant, Eleanor didn't enjoy little children and felt that motherhood did not suit her.

Franklin, who had been admitted to the bar although he didn't graduate from law school, had found work with a New York City law firm but, like Eleanor in her role as a mother, he was dissatisfied. It was time for Franklin to find his niche. With the Roosevelt name prominent in the political realm, it was only a matter of time before Franklin would explore opportunities in that direction.

Chapter Three

Politics and Infidelity

"Rules are not necessarily sacred; principles are."

—Franklin D. Roosevelt

Franklin didn't like being a lawyer and with a family example so immediately at hand, it didn't take much persuasion when, in 1910, representatives from New York's Democratic Party contacted him to suggest that he give politics a go. He had the name, the money, and the zeal to be a political candidate and when he ran for the state senate in Dutchess County, he won the election by one thousand votes in a district that was largely Republican. However, the Republican Party was split between conservative and progressive factions, opening the way for a challenger.

Although he was a Democrat, and former President Roosevelt was a Republican, both Roosevelts firmly felt that if American society was to provide equal opportunity for all citizens, the government needed to play its part. Too much power concentrated in any group was a threat to the individual. Franklin was an advocate for the Republican farmers in the district, and in 1912, he was re-elected. Fortune was already smiling upon him, and his networking contacts were paying off.

By supporting Woodrow Wilson's campaign for the presidency in the 1912 election, Franklin won when Wilson did. Wilson appreciated the support of the political newcomer, and his Secretary of the Navy offered Franklin the position of Assistant Secretary of the Navy, a position that Theodore Roosevelt had also held under President McKinley before he won the vice-presidential position. For Franklin, whose love of sailing easily translated into an affection for the Navy, the assignment was ideally suited. Franklin went to work overseeing the daily business of his department with the help of Louis Howe, a journalist who would become his friend and later, his political advisor.

Franklin's enthusiasm for an expanded Navy earned him the support of Navy personnel. Franklin saw how much the Americans needed to improve the Navy, a lesson that he learned by paying attention to what was going on in Europe, where World War I was raging. The German submarine was a new form of technology, and Franklin recognized its potential. As the Allies were on the receiving end of submarine warfare, he supported the idea of constructing a mine barrier from Scotland to Norway in order to counteract the German threat to Allied shipping in the North Sea.

Wilson had run for reelection on the theme of maintaining American neutrality in the global conflict, but Franklin opposed that stance and believed that the United States needed to enter the war. In 1917, he got his wish as the doughboys of the U.S. joined the fight on the side of Great Britain and France. Roosevelt's position had domestic relevance as well as, in order to win approval of budgets, he learned how to negotiate with members of Congress.

Franklin remained in his post for the demobilization of the American troops and was resistant to any intentions of dismantling the Navy. World War I had disillusioned the world and even the victors shrank from the thought that they might have to fight again. Franklin, although he wanted the Navy to be prepared to defend the nation in another military threat, was also in favor of President Wilson's belief that the League of Nations could prevent a second global war. The hope was forlorn, as the United States rejected Wilson's dream of a League of Nations, and the seeds for World War II were already planted in the grounds of a devastated and embittered Germany.

But for Franklin Roosevelt, his time as the Assistant Secretary of the Navy provided a valuable apprenticeship for the future when he would serve as the commander-in-chief, with all branches of the military under his control. He could not have known in 1918 when he crossed the English Channel to inspect American naval facilities in Great Britain and France, that his meeting with Winston Churchill, then serving in the British government, would not be the last time that the two men would meet as representatives of their country during a war with the Germans.

While Franklin worked to strengthen the Navy, and while the world was at war, his private home was not entirely at peace either. In 1916, he had begun an affair with Eleanor's social secretary, Lucy Mercer, who had worked in a dress shop until Eleanor hired her in 1914. She blended in well with the family and Eleanor was fond of her. But the summer of 1916 saw Eleanor and the children on vacation while Franklin remained in Washington. Shortly after, Lucy Mercer's employment with the Roosevelts ended, whether because Eleanor fired her or because she chose to leave is unknown. In 1917, Mercer enlisted in the U.S. Navy and was assigned to work in Franklin's office. There was gossip in Washington D.C. regarding the frequency with which the young woman and the Assistant Secretary of the Navy were seen together. Alice Roosevelt Longworth, former President Theodore Roosevelt's outspoken daughter, invited the couple to dine with her. She approved of the affair because she felt that Franklin deserved a good time. Her reason? "He was married to Eleanor."

After Franklin had gone to Europe to inspect the naval facilities, he returned home with pneumonia. While he was ill, Eleanor unpacked his suitcases and found the love letters that Mercer had written to him. Eleanor offered him a divorce and Franklin was strongly tempted to accept. His advisor Louis Howe warned him that divorce would have a disastrous effect on his political ambitions. But it was his mother who put her foot down. Sara Delano Roosevelt threatened to disinherit her son and leave him without a dollar if he divorced his wife. Franklin bowed to their will and vowed that he would not see his mistress again, a promise that would prove impossible to keep.

The damage to the marriage was done, but the union remained. Eleanor, who had given birth to six children over a decade (one, named for his father, had died in infancy) did not seek comfort in the intimacy of the marital bond, and she pursued her interest in politics and social work.

Despite the disillusionment, the Roosevelt marriage would form a powerful bond when the nation called upon them to lead; Eleanor would prove to be a dynamic political influence on her husband. On the horizon was another obstacle, one which would alter Franklin's life to a greater extent than his infidelity, and Eleanor more than anyone would be the means of his restoration.

Chapter Four

Roosevelt, the Paraplegic

"The perfect naturalness with which the children accepted his limitations though they had always known him as an active person, helped him tremendously in his own acceptance of them."

—Eleanor Roosevelt

Despite his relative youth, Franklin Roosevelt was chosen to be the vice-presidential candidate in the election of 1920; his Wilson years had given him a broader profile than he would have had if he had remained a New York state senator. He had a name that was well known. But James Cox, the governor of Ohio, didn't have what was needed to defeat the Republican ticket of Warren G. Harding and Calvin Coolidge, even in the first election in which women could vote.

With no federal position, Roosevelt returned home to New York and his law practice. The summer after the presidential election, he went to the family cottage at Campobello Island in Canada after having visited a Boy Scout camp in New York. While sailing on his yacht, Roosevelt fell overboard into the water. When his lower back felt sore the next day, Franklin thought a swim would help, but that solution failed and by the third day, his legs were weakening and his body was no longer able to support his weight. A slight breeze upon his skin was unbearable. Eleanor summoned doctors; one said that Roosevelt had a blood clot in the lower spinal cord, and that the cure was lumbar massages every day to promote circulation. The massages proved ineffective, and a second doctor diagnosed infantile paralysis or polio, an incurable disease at that time. This doctor said the massages might be making the symptoms worse, and he recommended hot baths instead.

The Roosevelts were mystified. Infantile paralysis was, as the name indicated, a disease that was known to afflict children, who typically were immune to it by the time they were four years old. The doctor explained that it wasn't that simple. To combat the condition, a person had to have a healthy immune system along with good overall health. Franklin, however, had often been ill as a child, and his recent career had included stress.

Roosevelt was determined to fight the disease, a decision that meant giving up his political career. He returned home to Hyde Park and began a regimen of physical therapy. Three times a day, he went swimming because, in the water, his legs could support his body. By the winter of 1921, the strength in his arms had returned, his lower back was improving, and his nervous system was functioning normally. In January 1922, he was fitted with braces on his legs, and spring saw him standing up with assistance. He set goals for himself, vowing that he would walk the quarter-mile length of his driveway, a goal that he was not able to accomplish.

But illness did not quash Roosevelt's spirit as he maintained a consistent exercise routine even when in the company of friends. Franklin thrived on the camaraderie of family and loved ones, and he refused to surrender to despair; while he was exercising, he continued his conversation with his guests while he moved. It was harder for his children, who had known him as an active and vigorous father, to see him afflicted by the disease, where movement was a struggle and standing on his own impossible. But their father drew upon their presence and they learned to become a part of his determination to overcome the limitations of polio.

Friends, too, wanted to see Franklin overcome the debilitation of the disease and one of them, having heard of someone who had benefitted from the rich mineral content of the waters of Warm Springs, Georgia, informed Franklin, who went there in 1924 to find out for himself. The water did not cure him, but he continued to go, and when, in 1926, Warm Springs was in troubled financial straits, its most famous client bought the facility and turned it into a rehabilitation center for people with polio. He would continue to bath there throughout his life, even during his presidential career.

But the effects of polio, despite Roosevelt's upbeat approach and his diligent exercise, did not vanish. Franklin had to decide how to handle that, and whether he was going to return to politics or allow his illness to curtail his ambitions, which in the early 1920s had dared to entertain thoughts of the presidency. His mother felt that he should retire from public life; she disliked the visibility of politics, and since Franklin was now handicapped, she thought it more suitable for him to accept his limitations and live a retired life, out of sight.

Eleanor, despite the emotional estrangement caused by his infidelity with Lucy Mercer, addressed his physical condition in a very different manner than that of her mother-in-law. She opposed any notion that he should concede defeat and abandon his ambitions. Louis Howe, Roosevelt's advisor, agreed.

Returning to the spotlight was daunting. In 1924, Franklin made an appearance at the Democratic Convention in support of New York's Governor Al Smith. The public knew that he had withdrawn from society, but news of his illness and the effects were not widespread. Roosevelt found, somewhat to his surprise, that the public did not reject him for his physical condition. That support buoyed his conviction that politics was his element.

Smith appreciated Roosevelt's support and encouraged him to run for governor of New York in 1928, even though Smith didn't win the presidency. Roosevelt won by a very narrow margin, and he was able to pursue reform-minded social programs. When he ran for re-election in 1930, he had an unusual ally to back him up. The stock market crash of 1929 had pounded the American economy, leading to the Great Depression. It was a winning formula, and Roosevelt convincingly won re-election.

The country was limping under the catastrophic burden of unemployment, failing banks, foreclosures, and the feeling of hopelessness. Franklin knew very well what it was like to limp but keep going. He had never come to terms with his physical weakness, but he had figured out how to accommodate it without surrendering. He had designed a wheelchair that could move easily inside buildings. Taking a dining room chair, he replaced its legs with wheels that resembled those of a bicycle. With his invention, he could make his way down the narrow corridors of a house.

That worked for inside, but campaigning was another matter entirely. Roosevelt didn't want to present himself as a man who was dependent or limited. He had to figure out a way to walk, no small matter for a paraplegic. By leaning on someone with one arm and holding a cane in the other hand, Roosevelt learned how to move his hips and legs in a swinging motion and walk short distances. He manipulated stairs by supporting his weight with his arms, wobbling from one step to the next.

Franklin's body had seen defeat, but his spirit was unvanquished. For downtrodden Americans, he was a reminder that, although they were down, they were not out. As Eleanor said, "You gain strength, courage and confidence by every experience in which you really stop to look fear in the face. You are able to say to yourself, 'I have lived through this horror. I can take the next thing that comes along.' You must do the thing you think you cannot do."

Chapter Five

FDR Offers Americans a New Deal

"I took economic courses in college for four years and everything I was taught was wrong."

—Franklin D. Roosevelt

Herbert Hoover had virtually no chance of being re-elected president in 1932. His approach to the Great Depression which had stricken the country in 1929 and showed no signs of ending, was to do nothing and let the crisis run its course. The incumbent president was an easy target, and Franklin realized that he just needed to avoid making mistakes in order to beat him.

By 1931, American industrial production was cut in half. Bread lines and soup kitchens were often the only food that some people would have for a meal. Drought hit the heartland, and American farmers, facing crashing food prices, couldn't afford to harvest what they'd planted and had no choice but to let the crops rot in the fields. Shantytowns, populated by people who had lost their homes and had no jobs, sprouted up on the outskirts of the cities and were called Hoovervilles for the president, Herbert Hoover, who, in the eyes of many Americans, was doing nothing to ease the crisis. Hoover gave no specifics on just what he could do to alleviate the situation, leading some political experts to doubt that he had the ability to understand the problems facing the country or solve them.

When Roosevelt accepted the Democratic nomination for president at the convention in Chicago, his speech hinted at his plans. "I pledge you, I pledge myself to a new deal for the American people. . . . This is more than a political campaign. It is a call to arms."

The election results demonstrated just how fully Americans had lost faith in the Republican Party. Franklin won overwhelmingly and so did the Democrats, winning both the House of Representatives and the Senate, which would be significant for Roosevelt as he took over the helm of the listing ship of state. |

Winning 57% of the vote, carrying all but six states, Franklin's victory changed American politics by giving clout to organized labor, ethnic Americans, and African-Americans as well as reshaping the Democratic Party. But until he took the oath of office, Roosevelt refused to step in to help Hoover, although the president asked to meet with the president-elect so that they could join forces to calm investors. Franklin said, "It's not my baby," as the economy continued to come apart. By the time Hoover was out of office, the banking system was collapsing, and most of them had closed. Thirteen million Americans were out of work.

The president who couldn't use his legs intended to hit the ground running. He resolved, in his first hundred days in office, to propose to Congress measures that would give business and agriculture the impetus they needed to function, assist people who were out of work and in danger of losing their homes and farms, and bring about reform.

In his inaugural speech, Roosevelt proclaimed that the only thing Americans had to fear was fear itself. There was plenty of reason for fear. On the day after his March 4, 1933, inauguration, he declared a bank holiday. Calling Congress into a special session on March 9, Roosevelt proposed the Emergency Banking Act, following by the Glass-Steagall Act and the Federal Deposit Insurance Corporation, measures that were all designed to restore confidence in the nation's banks.

The Federal Trade Commission received new regulatory powers and was able to provide relief for the millions of Americans who were having difficulty paying their mortgages. The Reconstruction Finance Corporation, which had been a program under President Hoover, was expanded to become a major source of funding for industry and railroads. He also continued Hoover's relief program assisting the unemployed, giving it a new name, the Federal Emergency Relief Administration.

The farms were in trouble, and that made them a priority. Roosevelt set up the Agricultural Adjustment Administration, which paid farmer not to plant and to cut their herds; the purpose was to force higher process for commodities. Roosevelt's favorite program was the

Civilian Conservation Corps which put young men to work on projects in rural areas.

The overall economy's plight was in the hands of the National Industrial Recovery Act, which insisted that industries set consistent standards within specific categories; minimum prices, agreements holding off on competition, and production restrictions were among NIRA's requirements. NIRA pumped $3.3 billion into economic stimulus programs like the Public Works Administration. The Tennessee Valley Authority, which built dams and power stations that could control flooding and bring modernization to the agriculture and homes of the region, eased the poverty of the people living there. And in 1934, the Securities and Exchange Commission was established with the purpose of regulating Wall Street.

Another of Roosevelt's acts was to repeal Prohibition. Not only was it legal to drink alcohol, but taxing alcohol provided the federal government with a new source of revenue. Roosevelt levied higher taxes on wealthy Americans, established new controls over banks and public utilities, and created a work relief program for the many who still didn't have jobs. Social Security also passed.

But in 1935, the Supreme Court ruled that NIRA was unconstitutional. Eventually, in Roosevelt's second term, Congress would pass the Fair Labor Standards Act, the last significant legislation of the New Deal's domestic reforms.

Roosevelt's bold programs poured money and adrenaline into the country's moribund economy, but the nation's business sector began to oppose his efforts. Roosevelt took the U.S. off the gold standard, an act which the businesses found appalling. They didn't like the government's support of labor and unions. They also didn't like the deficits in the budget that arose as a result of the spending. By 1935, the results were showing some admittedly limited progress. "The country needs and, unless I mistake its temper, the country demands bold, persistent experimentation," Roosevelt wrote. "It is common sense to take a method and try it; if it fails, admit it frankly and try another. But above all, try something."

The rich and powerful might not have liked what he was doing, but the voters did, and he was re-elected in 1936. Infused with the mandate of his election, Roosevelt tried to increase the size of the Supreme Court to fifteen because the justices' rulings sought to undo the New Deal legislation that he'd put forth.

He didn't win his battle to pack the court, but what he was winning was the loyalty of the American voter. There were still eight million people unemployed, and the economy was far from where it needed to be, but the common people saw in the Ivy League, patrician Roosevelt someone who was willing to fight for them. Franklin reveled in the hostility of the Republicans who were suspicious of the administration and its intentions, and he was unperturbed when he was compared to Lenin and Marx for his actions. The venom of those who opposed him, however, helped to support the public view that

Roosevelt was the man defending the working classes against those who sought to keep them powerless. FDR let the accusations against him go on, knowing that his detractors were demonstrating how intractable they could be even when the country was still struggling to get back on its economic feet. The Wagner Act gave labor unions a dynamic burst of political influence, and they used their new clout to support the president who had supported them. One worker, trying to explain his confidence in President Roosevelt, said, that FDR was the first "man in the White House who knows that my boss is a son of a bitch."

Chapter Six

Eleanor, the First Lady

"Do what you feel in your heart to be right—for you'll be criticized anyway. You'll be damned if you do, and damned if you don't."

—Eleanor Roosevelt

The woman who was daunted by her mother-in-law, who felt incapable of measuring up to traditional standards of female beauty such as the ones her mother had represented, who saw her marriage compromised by her husband's infidelity, would become the First Lady against whom all subsequent First Ladies have been measured. When Roosevelt entered the White House in 1933, his physical condition made him dependent upon his wife; she was, they both understood, his "eyes and ears."

Eleanor had had a social conscience since her debutante days and had taken her fiancée, Franklin Roosevelt, with her when she visited the garment district of New York early in their romance. However, after he was stricken with polio, he didn't want the public to see him in a wheelchair, struggling to maneuver inside buildings constructed at a time when handicapped accessibility was an unknown concept. Eleanor could go where he could not. That mobility would also navigate her political awakening, as she would support women's rights, civil rights, and labor to an extent that sometimes made her a political liability in Washington D.C., whose movers and shakers looked askance at the active First Lady who clearly did not heed the advice that a woman's place was in the home.

Eleanor's advice on how the nation's First Lady should conduct herself reveals both a sense of humor and a touch of cynicism. "Always be on time. Do as little talking as humanly possible. Lean back in the parade car so everybody can see the president."

Eleanor began her first term as First Lady by announcing that she would hold weekly meetings with female reporters to make the public aware of the White House activities during the nation's time of crisis. She was not afraid of stirring controversy with her words, in fact, she said, she was making the comments deliberately because the subjects needed to be discussed. She encouraged women to write to her with ideas for her monthly column in the *Women's Home Companion*. In less than a year, 300,000 Americans heeded her call and sent her their views.

From the beginning, Eleanor Roosevelt saw her role as one of substance as she turned the Lincoln bedroom into a study. She pressed her husband to name women to posts of influence in the New Deal programs that he had initiated.

Eleanor insisted on leading by example, even when her methods displeased her husband. In order to conduct a no-frills lifestyle at the White House, she enlisted Cornell

University's home economics faculty to advise on the preparation of nutritious meals that didn't cost a lot of money. Those meals proved to be tasteless. So she hired a woman named Henrietta Nesbitt to plan the White House meals. President Roosevelt complained that, even though he wanted chicken a la king to be served as the meal for his fourth inauguration, he was given chicken salad. The news of the White House's lack of culinary distinction spread and guests knew that they should eat at home before showing up for dinner at the Roosevelts. The first couple was not known for their grand hospitality.

Even though she had enemies, the First Lady refused Secret Service protection. She sought economic solutions to the poverty of a West Virginia coal town and showed up not only to help but also to socialize, taking part in square dances with the miners. Her advocacy revealed that some of the nation's most vulnerable citizens were women and minorities. She chaired the White House Conference on the Emergency Needs of Women because she had noticed that government programs failed to take the problems of unemployed women seriously.

Eleanor Roosevelt's views on civil rights were ahead of her time. When she attended the Southern Conference for Human Welfare, she sat next to an African-American, but she had to move because Alabama's racial policies forbade white and black people to sit next to each other. Eleanor had the distance measured between the white section and the black section. She then placed her chair exactly in the middle.

Her views were also distinctly at odds with mainstream thought in Washington D.C., which was racially segregated at the time. In 1940, the request by Howard University to have African-American singer Marian Anderson perform at the Daughters of the American Revolution Auditorium, the largest auditorium in the nation's capital, was denied. The donors who had funded the building of the auditorium stipulated that only white performers could appear on stage. Eleanor Roosevelt had been granted membership in the DAR in 1932, but she was not one of the powerhouses in the organization. But when the DAR failed to recognize Anderson's talent and worth, Eleanor resigned from the organization, writing that they had been given an opportunity to lead in an enlightened way, but had failed to do so.

Instead, she chose another way to honor the singer. She invited Anderson to sing at the White House when Great Britain's King George VI and Queen Elizabeth came to the United States. She also agreed to present a medal to Anderson at the National Association for the Advancement of Colored People's national convention.

Eleanor didn't do anything in half measures. Harold Ickes, the Secretary of the Interior, agreed with the First Lady that an outdoor concert at the Lincoln Memorial would be an ideal way to celebrate Anderson's musical talent while promoting cultural events. Roosevelt gave his approval for the concert.

On April 9, 1939, the Marian Anderson concert had an audience of 75,000 people, with thousands more listening on the radio. The radio announcer's version of why the concert was being held was not entirely accurate, "Marian Anderson is singing this public concert at the Lincoln Memorial because she was unable to get an auditorium to accommodate the tremendous audience that wishes to hear her." But by denying Anderson permission to sing, the DAR unwittingly set the stage for her groundbreaking performance that would ultimately serve as a monumental civil rights victory.

The concert began with an introduction by Secretary Ickes, who introduced the performer by asserting that there was no color line for genius; the concert ended with Anderson's encore performance of *Nobody Knows the Trouble I've Seen.* As First Lady, Eleanor Roosevelt understood that both the introduction and the song title were absolutely true.

Chapter Seven

The Arsenal of Democracy

"We must be the great arsenal of democracy. For us this is an emergency as serious as war itself. We must apply ourselves to our task with the same resolution, the same sense of urgency, the same spirit of patriotism and sacrifice as we would show were we at war."

—Franklin D. Roosevelt

Engrossed in their internal problems and struggling with an economy that remained stalled, Americans preferred to ignore the worsening situation in Europe. In 1933, the year that Franklin Roosevelt took office as president of the United States, Adolf Hitler had been named chancellor of Germany. Keenly aware of the international situation, Roosevelt's America was committed to neutrality, but after the Nazis had taken control of France, Great Britain was left to fight alone, and Roosevelt favored providing the British with military aid.

The war abroad influenced Franklin's decision when it was time for the election of 1940. Ever since George Washington, American presidents had honored the tradition of serving a maximum of two terms. But Franklin had confided in close friends that if circumstances in Europe continued to appear dire, he would run for a third term. France was conquered by German in the spring of 1940 and that made up Franklin's mind, if indeed he had considered not running. Not all Democrats wanted him to run, including his own Vice President John Garner. However, Roosevelt's new vice-presidential candidate Henry Wallace, the Secretary of Commerce, was firmly supportive of New Deal policies, even though he was a former Republican.

Knowing of the opposition within his party, Roosevelt had the convention moved to Chicago, where the Democratic party machine could be relied upon to come through for him and would not be overly scrupulous in doing so. He sent a message that he did not intend to run unless his party drafted him, freeing the delegates to vote for whichever candidate they chose. A voice from the loudspeaker—which the Chicago party machinery controlled—called out they wanted Roosevelt. The delegates nominated Roosevelt with 946 votes on the first ballot.

The year 1940 in the United States was somewhat overshadowed by what was going on across the ocean. The Lend-Lease program, which provided military and economic aid to the Allied Powers fighting the Nazis, was Roosevelt's way of supporting America's friends in a war that he knew the United States would not be able to avoid for much longer.

It was certain that Americans didn't want war, especially a global one. Memories were still vivid of the First World War, but Roosevelt prepared the nation in a way that Woodrow Wilson, who was president during

World War I, had not. Roosevelt got a jump on things by expanding war production before the United States was caught in the conflagration, having begun the rearmament process in 1938. He also initiated the military draft in 1940. Roosevelt was ever vigilant in gauging his country's mood, just as he carefully and cannily paid attention to what was going on abroad. But internally, American isolationism had spokesmen like Charles Lindbergh, the famed aviator, who criticized Roosevelt for taking sides against Germany instead of maintaining neutrality.

Franklin, in his fireside chats, had maintained communication with the public who listened to his words on the radio. Beginning in 1933, he had used radio to communicate with the American public as his voice entered their living rooms. That was the medium he used on December 29, 1940, when he explained why the United States was providing Lend-Lease assistance to the forces who were fighting the Nazis. America, he said, supported freedom. "The people of Europe who are defending themselves do not ask us to do their fighting. They ask us for the implements of war, the planes, the tanks, the guns, the freighters which will enable them to fight for their liberty and for our security. Emphatically we must get these weapons to them in sufficient volume and quickly enough, so that we and our children will be saved the agony and suffering of war which others have had to endure."

The war seemed to escalate in 1941. The Nazis invaded the Soviet Union in June, which led Roosevelt to include the Soviets in America's Lend-Lease program. When a German submarine fired on a U.S. destroyer, he said that the Navy would escort Allied convoys; if German vessels entered the U. S. Navy zone, American ships would "shoot on sight." This policy won the approval of Americans who may not have realized that it amounted to declaring naval war against the Germans.

July saw Roosevelt instruct Henry Stimson, Secretary of War, to begin what was called the "Victory Program" to start the planning for America's military involvement. This preliminary step gave estimates that the military would need for mobilization the nations' human, industrial, and logistical resources to defeat the Axis powers of Germany and Japan. Japanese aggression was making Americans uneasy, although at the time there was no direct threat to the United States.

But when Japan and China went to war in 1937, and the U.S.S. Panay was bombed while it was evacuating Americans from Nanjing, American sympathies were with the Chinese. The peace between the two countries was an uneasy one, but Japan apologized for the bombing, and the apology was officially accepted. As Japan signed pacts with Germany and the Vichy Government in France, the United States responded by placing an embargo on exports to the Japanese, freezing Japanese assets in American banks, and sending supplies to assist China. Japan felt threatened by the United States, but the consensus in the U.S. was that Japan lacked the military force necessary to mount an attack.

In August 1941, Roosevelt met with British Prime Minister Winston Churchill, something they would do ten more times, with the purpose of drafting the Atlantic Charter, which outlined the goals endorsed by the Allied powers for wartime and the post-war period. According to the plan, not only would American aid to the Allies be increased, but the United States would have five million soldiers ready to be deployed overseas in 1943.

Americans recognized that they were living in perilous times, but they still hoped to avoid entering the war in Europe. No one gave any real thought to a war in the Pacific, although by early December, Roosevelt and his government were paying close attention to Japanese troop movements in French Indochina, movements which the Japanese claimed were only precautionary. On December 6, 1941, Roosevelt sent a message to Japan's emperor, and the government waited for a response.

Chapter Eight

The United States Enters War

"Yesterday, December 7, 1941, a date which will live in infamy, the United States of America was suddenly and deliberately attacked by naval and air forces of the Empire of Japan. We will gain the inevitable triumph, so help us God."

—Franklin D. Roosevelt

As 1941 began, the American ambassador to Japan observed that he was hearing talk that if matters didn't go well, the Japanese planned a mass attack on Pearl Harbor. The ambassador concluded that, as he put it, "I rather guess that the boys in Hawaii are not precisely asleep." The Navy ignored his warning.

The world had, to its peril, ignored the aggressive of countries with an aim to showcase their military might against their neighbors. Europe was paying the price for those years as Hitler's armies rearranged the landscape. In the United States, Americans felt safe with their oceans to protect them and their ignorance to comfort them.

But Roosevelt had not buried his head in the sand, watching if not acting, as the bullying of nations escalated during a time when the world was so occupied with its economic plight that it failed to be vigilant. Early in Franklin's presidency, Congress had passed the Reciprocal Trade Agreements Act to bestow "most favored nation" status upon the countries with which the U.S. had trade agreements.

Roosevelt established official ties with the Soviet Union in 1933. He had continued the policy that Herbert Hoover had initiated to improve relations with Latin America, he withdrew the remaining American troops from the Caribbean, he accepted the Pan-American Conference stipulation that no country could claim the right to intervene in the affairs of another country, and he also accepted the decision by Mexico to nationalize its oil industry, despite internal dissent over the effect this would have on America.

Time passed, and Congress, between 1935 and 1939, passed five different Neutrality Acts. By 1940, Adolf Hitler conquered France, Belgium, the Netherlands, Norway and Denmark and, ravenous for more, he had begun his air war against the United Kingdom in preparation for an invasion. The Americans remained stubbornly isolationist, and Roosevelt could not buck their will. He could and did, however, lay the groundwork for support by providing the British with aid. Lend-Lease in 1941 provided allies with access to U.S. arms and supplies; that amount would eventually amount to more than $50 billion, well above the $7 billion that Congress originally appropriated.

When the British did not fall to the Nazi air assault, Hitler ordered German submarines to attack shipping in the North Atlantic. He also invaded the Soviet Union. In response, Roosevelt extended the Lend-Lease provisions to the Soviets and sent the American Navy to patrol the North Atlantic and provide escort for British ships. With American ships ready to fire on German submarines, a virtual state of war existed between the two nations by the fall of 1941.

The clock was running out on American disengagement in the global state of war. At 7:55 a.m. Hawaii time, 353 Imperial Japanese fighter planes, launched from six aircraft carriers, attacked the U.S. naval base at Pearl Harbor. Eight American battleships were damaged, and four were sunk; 188 aircraft were destroyed. The attack killed 2,403 Americans and wounded more than 1,000 others. Japanese losses were light in comparison: 64 men were killed and one was captured; 29 aircraft and five midget submarines were lost. But the massive attack also included strikes against Guam, Wake Island, Malaya, Singapore, Hong Kong, and the Philippines.

Despite the devastating two-hour attack, the Pacific Fleet was not destroyed. The Japanese intention was to block the U.S. from interfering with their plans to strike the Asian territories of the Americans, British, and Dutch. But the Japanese failed to hit the base's oil storage depots, repair shops, or shipyard and submarine docks. Also, none of the aircraft carriers were at the base; some were delivering planes to Midway Island and Wake Island while others had returned to the mainland. This would prove pivotal for the U.S. Navy, which would be able to recover relatively swiftly from the surprise attack.

But the average American, learning of the assault, took no comfort and was shocked by what Japan had done to Pearl Harbor. On December 8, Roosevelt asked Congress to declare war against Japan. He said, "No matter how long it may take us to overcome this premeditated invasion, the American people in their righteous might will win through to absolute victory. I believe that I interpret the will of the Congress and of the people when I assert that we will not only defend ourselves to the uttermost but will make it very certain that this form of treachery shall never again endanger us."

With only one dissenting vote, Congress approved the resolution. Three days later, Germany and Italy declared war on the U.S. America ended 1941 as a full-scale participant in World War II. While the Allies were relieved at having a fresh partner in the conflict which was exhausting their resources, the truth was that the United States was not prepared, and its military forces soon experienced the overwhelming force of Axis power. Nearly one million tons of Allied shipping were sent to the bottom of the Atlantic Ocean, sunk by the German submarines, early in 1942. Japanese victories claimed islands in Asia as they triumphed over America and its allies in the Pacific.

War strategy had already been determined before the U.S. entered the war; Roosevelt was determined to be a full commander-in-chief for this global battle and not to solely rely, as his World War I predecessor Woodrow Wilson had done, on the generals. The Americans were designated to hold the Pacific against Japan while the Allies battled Hitler in Europe. In May 1942, the U.S. Navy defeated Japan at Midway Island, bringing the Japanese advance to a stop. Working together, the British and American naval convoys were able to limit the effects of German submarines in the North Atlantic.

By the end of the year, Great Britain and the United States launched an offensive against Germany in North Africa. The following year, 1943, saw the United States achieving victory against the Japanese at Guadalcanal, Tarawa, and Bougainville, but at a terrible price in casualties. To win victory at Tarawa, which consisted of 300 acres of land, 3,000 Americans lost their lives.

The year of 1943 also saw a turn in the Allied fortunes in Europe. The British and Americans finished their campaign for North Africa. The Soviets were able to turn back the Nazis at the battle of Stalingrad. The Russians had suffered, and Premier Joseph Stalin wanted the Allies to attack France so that Germany would be forced to move troops from its eastern to its western front. But Churchill's plan to invade Italy won the day, although the leaders promised that they would invade France in 1944.

Chapter Nine

The Death of the Longest Serving President

"The President slept away this afternoon. He did his job to the end as he would want to do."

—Eleanor Roosevelt

In early June, 1944, Supreme Allied Commander Dwight D. Eisenhower was closely monitoring the weather forecasts. He had planned the invasion of Normandy, the massive advance of soldiers and equipment that was designed to defeat the Nazis, for June 5, but the forecast made him change the date to June 6, D-Day. Within a week, more than 326,000 troops, 50,000 vehicles, and 100,000 tons of equipment were in Europe with the intention of defeating the Nazis.

The Battle of Normandy occupied the summer of 1944, but by late August, northern France had been freed from Nazi control and Paris was liberated. The Allies were ready to invade Germany and join forces with the Soviet Army which was coming from the east. The end of the war in Europe was within sight. The Allies could predict the eventual fall of Germany. But despite Allied victories in Asia which gave the Americans control over islands that could be used for the launching of bombers against the Japanese, the invasion of Japan loomed as a fearsome obstacle before victory could be achieved.

By the end of 1944, it was clear that the Allies would win, although victory was still months away. But the alliance that was winning World War II was fraught with tensions over what would happen after the war. When the Atlantic Charter was written in 1942, Roosevelt had called the coalition of the 26 nations that supported its goals the United Nations. His intention was for the world to join forces to pursue peace and cooperation instead of war and hostility.

When President Roosevelt, Prime Minister Churchill, and Premier Stalin met in Yalta in February 1945, the Allied leaders were assuming their positions for a post-war world. Russia had sacrificed greatly in the war and in return, Stalin expected to control a section of Europe which would answer to Moscow and not to British or American ideals of freedom and self-determination. In exchange for his promise to allow free elections in eastern Europe, Stalin would receive the territory that Russia had lost to Japan in the Russo-Japanese War of 1904-1905. The Allies agreed that they would only accept unconditional surrender from Germany. The United States, Great Britain, the Soviet Union and France would divide Germany into sections; each of the Allied nations would occupy a zone.

The leaders agreed to meet again in April, with the intention of creating a United Nations. Roosevelt was an optimist by nature, and he believed that Stalin would keep the promises he had made at Yalta regarding free elections in eastern Europe, but the American Ambassador to the Soviet Union sent a cable a month after Yalta that presented a different viewpoint. Ambassador Averill Harriman told Roosevelt that "We must come clearly to realize that the Soviet program is the establishment of totalitarianism, ending personal liberty and democracy as we know it."

Earlier in his presidency, Roosevelt might have recognized the truth about Soviet ambitions. There was no disguising his failing health at the Yalta Conference. He had won the election to an unprecedented fourth term as president in 1944 even though his health was compromised by coronary artery disease, atherosclerosis, congestive heart failure, and high blood pressure. In addition, he looked exhausted, and his energy was ebbing. His doctors ordered rest. Franklin's physician set a schedule of two hours of rest each day and no visitors intent on business during lunch. Roosevelt had already been hiding the truth about his health from the public before the election when he instructed the Office of Censorship to prohibit any information about his physical status to appear in the media.

But word had eked out, some of it by Roosevelt himself. When he appeared before Congress to inform the members of the results from Yalta, he was seated. He explained, "I hope that you will pardon me for this unusual posture of sitting down during the presentation of what I want to say . . . it makes it a lot easier for me not to have to carry about ten pounds of steel around on the bottom of my legs."

Concerned about his health, daughter Anna Roosevelt, who had moved into the White House to help her father while Eleanor was busy with her social projects, had arranged for Lucy Mercer, Roosevelt's former mistress, to visit him. Despite his promise to his wife, Roosevelt and Mercer had remained in contact during the decades since Eleanor had found the secret love letters that revealed her husband's affair.

To restore his health, Roosevelt returned to Warm Springs, Georgia, which had been his sanctuary for much of his life after contracting polio. Mercer was with him at "the little White House" in April. She asked him to have his portrait painted, and he complied. Around 1:00 pm on April 12, 1945, Roosevelt was reading a speech he would be delivering when he commented that he had a terrific pain in the back of his head. He collapsed in his chair, unconscious. When a doctor was summoned, he realized that Roosevelt had suffered a massive cerebral hemorrhage. By 3:30 pm, the president was pronounced dead. The artist, Elizabeth Shoumatoff, rushed Mercer away from the residence to avoid disclosure and publicity, and the affair would remain a secret to the public until the 1960s.

Not only the United States but also the world was stunned at the news that Roosevelt was gone. British Prime Minister Winston Churchill felt as if the news of the president's death struck him like a physical blow. Premier Joseph Stalin, whose relationship with Roosevelt was a warm and cordial one, described the president as a "far-sighted and liberal leader."

As the flag-draped coffin containing Roosevelt's body made its way back to Washington, D.C., thousands of Americans stood by the train tracks to pay their respects to the leader who had governed for so long. There was a funeral service at the White House on April 14 and on the following day, Roosevelt's body was buried in the rose garden of the Roosevelt family home in Hyde Park, New York.

On the day of the president's death, at 5:30 pm, Eleanor told Vice President Harry Truman that Roosevelt was dead. When Truman asked if there was anything he could do for her, Eleanor replied, "Is there anything we can do for you? For you are the one in trouble now."

Less than a month after Roosevelt's death, President Truman dedicated May 8, Victory in Europe Day, to his memory. Harry Truman ascended to the office of the presidency at a time of immense international strife, yet he and Roosevelt had met only twice during the 82 days that Truman was the vice president. He admitted to reporters after taking the oath of office that he needed help, "Boys, if you ever pray, pray for me now." He kept Roosevelt's Cabinet in place, and Secretary of War Henry Stimson told him that the United States had a top-secret weapon. On April 25, he learned just how powerful that weapon, the atomic bomb, was. Stalin, thanks to his spies, had known about the existence of the bomb before Truman.

Europe was won, and Hitler was dead, but Japan had not surrendered. Experts estimated that invading mainland Japan could take another year and as many as half a million American casualties. On August 6, Truman ordered the dropping of the atomic bomb on Hiroshima, followed three days later by a bomb on Nagasaki. Japan surrendered on August 9, 1945.

Franklin D. Roosevelt had not lived to see the victorious end of the war that he had fought. But he believed that the Allies would win because he believed that ultimately, the United States and its ideals would triumph over economic adversity, enemy aggression, and forces hostile to democracy, just as he had triumphed over polio to become one of country's most highly regarded presidents.

Conclusion

"Men will thank God on their knees a hundred years from now that Franklin D. Roosevelt was in the White House."

—The New York Times

The 1930s represented a time when the poisonous seeds of destiny were doomed to ripen into harvest. World War I had left Germany seething beneath the debt of reparations it could not repay to the Allied victors who were determined to see the Germans punished. When the collapse of economic prosperity entered the equation, citizens all over the world were bewildered as they searched for reasons why this fate had befallen them. Germany sought a return to its imperial grandeur as it constructed a war machine based on the conviction that the Jews were at fault. Other nations, seeking power and security beyond their borders, opted for martial solutions to internal problems. Nazism, fascism, and communism grew as people searched for answers that, however toxic, assured them that they deserved better.

In the United States, stricken though it was by the economic collapse that began in October 1929, Americans voted their hope and not their fear when, in the 1932 presidential election, they rallied for Franklin D. Roosevelt, a liberal, pedigreed New Yorker who believed that the United States could overcome its travail. Merely bringing a country out of a devastating financial collapse would make a president memorable, but FDR also led his nation to a successful resolution of a world war so punishing and deadly that it mocked the notion that its predecessor was the war to end all wars.

Roosevelt kept his country from the brink of financial ruin, and he preserved the United States, and the world, from the deadly vision of Nazi Germany. The federal government assumed the burden of revitalizing the banking system so that Americans could once again have confidence in the nation's financial institutions. His legislation gave labor unions the right to organize to protect the rights of workers, even though members of his class despised him for the concessions that he made to the working man and woman. The Harvard-educated Roosevelt with the upper-class accent fought so that ordinary men and women would have a place in the country.

He did not accomplish everything that would have rid the United States of all its ills. He did not fight segregation as fiercely as First Lady Eleanor would have liked him to do. His wife was a lightning rod for reform. Franklin, a pragmatist, heard her pleas for change, but he also had his finger on the pulse of an embattled country that feared the future. In order to assuage fear and bring reform, he was obliged to embolden the federal government to assume powers that it had not previously sought. The man whose legs were wasted by polio was the leader whose strength allowed him to balance the caution of the present with the needs of the future.

The Roosevelt coalition rebranded the Democratic Party into a community where the whites of the Deep South and the blacks of the urban North, where Jews, Protestants and Catholics, farmers and union workers, could voice their views and find representation in government.

The diversity of problems that he faced required a White House machine unlike anything the country had ever seen. He needed able and agile staff members who could help him draft policies to keep the country stable and safe. Supporters of a weak and limited central government were not pleased and have continued to fight the metamorphosis of the Executive Branch as we know it today, but for many historians, Franklin D. Roosevelt's changes were the alchemy that transformed the United States into a world power.

Printed in Great Britain
by Amazon